HomeBuilders *Couples Series* ®

⊲ **W9-BUE-674**

improving
Communication
in Your Marriage

By Dr. Gary and Barbara Rosberg

*"Unless the Lord
builds the house,
its builders
labor in vain"*
(Psalm 127:1a).

FAMILYLIFE™
Bringing Timeless Principles Home
Little Rock, Arkansas

Group
Loveland, Colorado

Group's R.E.A.L. Guarantee to you:

Every Group resource incorporates our R.E.A.L. approach to ministry—a unique philosophy that results in long-term retention and life transformation. It's ministry that's:

This is EARL. He's R.E.A.L. mixed up. (Get it?)

Relational	**Experiential**	**Applicable**	**Learner-based**
Because student-to-student interaction enhances learning and builds Christian friendships.	Because what students experience sticks with them up to 9 times longer than what they simply hear or read.	Because the aim of Christian education is to be both hearers and doers of the Word.	Because students learn more and retain it longer when the process is designed according to how they learn best.

Improving Communication in Your Marriage

Visit our Web site: **www.grouppublishing.com**

Credits
FamilyLife
Editor: David Boehi
Assistant Editor: Julie Denker

Group Publishing, Inc.
Editor: Matt Lockhart
Creative Development Editor: Paul Woods
Chief Creative Officer: Joani Schultz
Copy Editors: Bob Kretschman and Pamela Shoup
Art Director: Jenette L. McEntire
Cover Art Director: Jeff A. Storm
Computer Graphic Artist: Anita M. Cook
Cover Photographer: Tony Stone Images
Illustrator: Ken Jacobsen
Production Manager: Peggy Naylor

Unless otherwise noted, Scripture taken from the HOLY BIBLE, NEW INTERNATIONAL VERSION®. Copyright © 1973, 1978, 1984 by International Bible Society. Used by permission of Zondervan Publishing House. All rights reserved.

ISBN 0-7644-2236-7
20 19 18   09 08 07 06 05

Printed in the United States of America.

How to Let the Lord Build Your House
and not labor in vain

●

The HomeBuilders Couples Series®: A small-group Bible study dedicated to making your family all that God intended.

FamilyLife is a division of Campus Crusade for Christ International, an evangelical Christian organization founded in 1951 by Bill Bright. FamilyLife was started in 1976 to help fulfill the Great Commission by strengthening marriages and families and then equipping them to go to the world with the gospel of Jesus Christ. The FamilyLife Marriage Conference is held in most major cities throughout the United States and is one of the fastest-growing marriage conferences in America today. "FamilyLife Today," a daily radio program hosted by Dennis Rainey, is heard on hundreds of stations across the country. Information on all resources offered by FamilyLife may be obtained by contacting us at the address, telephone number, or World Wide Web site listed below.

Dennis Rainey, Executive Director
FamilyLife
P.O. Box 8220
Little Rock, AR 72221-8220
1-800-FL-TODAY
www.familylife.com

A division of Campus Crusade for Christ International
Bill Bright, Founder and President

IMPROVING COMMUNICATION IN YOUR MARRIAGE

About the Sessions

Each session in this study is composed of the following categories: Warm-Up, Blueprints, Wrap-Up, and HomeBuilders Project. A description of each of these categories follows:

Warm-Up (15 minutes)

 The purpose of Warm-Up is to help people unwind from a busy day and get to know each other better. Typically the first point in Warm-Up is an exercise that is meant to be fun while introducing the topic of the session. The ability to share in fun with others is important in building relationships. Another component of Warm-Up is the Project Report (except in Session One), which is designed to provide accountability for the HomeBuilders Project that is to be completed by couples between sessions.

Blueprints (60 minutes)

This is the heart of the study. In this part of each session, people answer questions related to the topic of study and look to God's Word for understanding. Some of the questions are to be answered by couples, in subgroups, or in the group at large. There are notes in the margin or instructions within a question that designate these groupings.

Wrap-Up (15 minutes)

This category serves to "bring home the point" and wind down a session in an appropriate fashion.

HomeBuilders Project (60 minutes)

This project is the unique application step in a HomeBuilders study. Before leaving a meeting, couples are encouraged to "Make a Date" to do this project prior to the next meeting. Each HomeBuilders Project contains three sections: 1) As a Couple—a brief exercise designed to get the date started in a fun way; 2) Individually—a section of questions for husbands and wives to answer separately; 3) Interact as a Couple—an opportunity for couples to share their answers with each other and to make application in their lives.

In addition to the above regular features, occasional activities are labeled "For Extra Impact." These are activities that generally provide a more active or visual way to make a particular point. Be mindful that people within a group have different learning styles. While most of what is presented is verbal, a visual or active exercise now and then helps engage more of the senses and appeals to people who learn best by seeing, touching, and doing.

About the Authors

Dr. Gary and Barbara Rosberg are America's Family Coaches. They speak at conferences including FamilyLife Marriage Conferences and "I Still Do" events. Gary is also a platform speaker for Promise Keepers and Focus on the Family's Life on the Edge Conferences for parents and adolescents. Gary is the founder of CrossTrainers, a group of five hundred men who meet weekly. Barbara coaches women in a series called A Woman's Legacy—reminding them of the incredible value of womanhood.

The Rosbergs host "America's Family Coaches LIVE," a nationally syndicated daily radio program. They also host a Saturday radio program on the award-winning WHO Radio. Gary has authored *Dr. Rosberg's Do-It-Yourself Relationship Mender* and co-authored *Guard Your Heart* and *The Five Love Needs of Men and Women* with Barbara.

The Rosbergs are both graduates of Drake University. Gary earned master's and doctorate degrees in counseling, and Barbara holds a bachelor's degree in fine arts.

Gary and Barbara have been married since 1975 and reside in West Des Moines, Iowa. They are the parents of two adult daughters. Missy is a college student studying communications, and Sarah lives in West Des Moines, Iowa with her husband, Scott.

For more information about the ministries of the Rosbergs' America's Family Coaches, contact us at:

America's Family Coaches
2540 106th Street, Suite 101
Des Moines, IA 50322
1-888-ROSBERG
www.americasfamilycoaches.com

Contents

Acknowledgments

We want to thank some of the best couples in the country who joined with us as we field-tested this material in our home. They include: Rick and Pat Holmertz, Larry and Tracy Long, Phil and Julie Pigneri, Dan and Tricia Vermeer, Scott and Jane Larson, and Al and Vicki Sheldon.

We also want to thank our daughters, Sarah and Missy, as well as our incredible son-in-law, Scott, who give us the love and encouragement to help others. Thank you for allowing us to live in the dividend years as we watch you walk with Jesus Christ and impact others for the Kingdom.

The ministry team at America's Family Coaches has lifted up our arms so that we are free to do what we do best: coach, encourage, and equip America's families with the proven game plan to excel in building strong relationships. We will match our team with any in the country!

With heartfelt love we dedicate this HomeBuilders Couples Series study to the two couples who taught us how to build our marriage: our parents. To John and Audrey Rosberg who celebrated fifty-four years of marriage before Dad went home to be with the Lord and to Jack and Colleen Bedford who have celebrated fifty-nine years and still counting! Thank you for all you have done to teach us how to love, honor, and cherish each other!

Foreword

Polls and surveys consistently show that the number one issue that cripples a married couple's relationship is communication. And it does not take much time for this problem to begin to show itself. Once those feelings of hyper-romance from courtship and engagement begin to fade, married couples often wake up to some cold realizations: We aren't talking like we once did. We're having more disagreements than we ever thought we would. And we don't know how to handle it.

In this study you will learn how to improve your communication—how to talk to each other, how to listen, how to "close the loop" in conflict, and much more. And you'll have fun learning, because you'll do it with other couples who face the same issues in their marriage.

I can't think of any better guides in this process than Gary and Barbara Rosberg. They've been friends of mine for many years and have spoken at more than one hundred FamilyLife Marriage Conferences. Gary has counseled thousands of couples, and with Barbara heads up America's Family Coaches ministry in Des Moines. They know that the principles in this study work—they've seen them transform their marriage, and they've seen them influence thousands to have the kind of relationship God desires for a married couple.

My prayer is that this study will begin a journey you will never end—a journey toward oneness in your marriage.

Dennis Rainey
Executive Director, FamilyLife

Introduction

When a man and woman are married, they stand before a room of witnesses and proclaim their commitment to a lifetime of love. They recite a sacred vow "to have and to hold...from this day forward...to love, honor, and cherish...for better, for worse...for richer, for poorer...in sickness and in health...as long as we both shall live."

It's a happy day, perhaps the happiest in their lives. And yet, once the honeymoon ends, once the emotions of courtship and engagement subside, many couples realize that "falling in love" and building a good marriage are two different things. Keeping those vows is much more difficult than they thought it would be.

Otherwise intelligent people who would not think of buying a car, investing money, or even going to the grocery store without some initial planning enter into marriage with no plan of how to make that relationship succeed.

But God has already provided the plan, a set of blueprints for building a truly God-honoring marriage. His plan is designed to enable a man and woman to grow together in a mutually satisfying relationship and then to reach out to others with the love of Christ. Ignoring this plan leads only to isolation and separation between husband and wife. It's a pattern evident in so many homes today: Failure to follow God's blueprints results in wasted effort, bitter disappointment, and, in far too many cases, divorce.

In response to this need in marriages today, FamilyLife has developed a series of small-group studies called the HomeBuilders Couples Series.

You could complete this study alone with your spouse, but we strongly urge you to either form or join a group of couples studying this material. You will find that the questions in each session not only help you grow closer to your spouse, but they help create a special environment of warmth and fellowship as you study together how to build the type of marriage you desire. Participating in a HomeBuilders group could be one of the highlights of your married life.

The Bible: Your Blueprints for a God-Honoring Marriage

You will notice as you proceed through this study that the Bible is used frequently as the final authority on issues of life and marriage. Although written thousands of years ago, this Book still speaks clearly and powerfully about the conflicts and struggles faced by men and women. The Bible is God's Word— his blueprints for building a God-honoring home and for dealing with the practical issues of living.

We encourage you to have a Bible with you for each session. For this series we use the New International Version as our primary reference. Another excellent translation is the New American Standard Bible.

Ground Rules

Each group session is designed to be enjoyable and informative—and nonthreatening. Three simple ground rules will help ensure that everyone feels comfortable and gets the most out of the experience:

1. Don't share anything that would embarrass your spouse.

2. You may pass on any question you don't want to answer.

3. If possible, plan to complete the HomeBuilders Project as a couple between group sessions.

A Few Quick Notes About Leading a HomeBuilders Group

1. Leading a group is much easier than you may think! A group leader in a HomeBuilders session is really a "facilitator." As a leader, your goal is simply to guide the group through the discussion questions. You don't need to teach the material—in fact, we don't want you to! The special dynamic of a HomeBuilders group is that couples teach themselves.

2. This material is designed to be used in a home study, but it also can be adapted for use in a Sunday school environment. (See page 105 for more information about this option.)

3. We have included a section of Leader's Notes in the back of this book. Be sure to read through these notes before leading a session; they will help you prepare.

4. For more material on leading a HomeBuilders group, be sure to get a copy of the *HomeBuilders Leader Guide*, by Drew and Kit Coons. This book is an excellent resource that provides helpful guidelines on how to start a study, how to keep discussion moving, and much more.

Understanding the Barriers to Communication

Understanding the barriers to communication is the first step toward building strong communication necessary for a healthy marriage.

W A R M • U P   15 M I N U T E S

Married Mishaps

Go around the room, introduce yourselves, and briefly answer one or both of the following questions (Remember, don't share anything negative or embarrassing!):

- What's the funniest miscommunication you've heard of in someone's marriage, either in real life, on TV, or in a book or a movie?

- What is one difference between you and your spouse that you're both able to laugh about?

Getting Connected

Pass your books around the room with each couple writing their names, phone numbers, and e-mail addresses.

NAME, PHONE, & E-MAIL

NAME, PHONE, & E-MAIL

NAME, PHONE, & E-MAIL

NAME, PHONE, & E-MAIL

NAME, PHONE, & E-MAIL

NAME, PHONE, & E-MAIL

BLUEPRINTS   60 MINUTES

Any two people building a marriage—whether they come from different cultures or different backgrounds—will face barriers in communicating effectively since they at least come from different families. Overcoming these barriers is part of the challenge of marriage. Unfortunately, many couples have never taken the time to analyze the communication barriers they face.

The Number-One Need

1. Couples everywhere indicate that the biggest need in their marriages is "improved communication." Why do you think good communication is such a problem?

If you have a large group, form smaller groups of about six people to answer the Blueprints questions. Unless otherwise noted, answer the questions in your sub-group. After finishing each section, take time for subgroups to share their answers with the whole group.

2. Why do you think good communication is vital to marriage?

HomeBuilders Principle:
How well you communicate can make or break your marriage.

Barriers to Communication

3. What barriers make it a challenge for couples to communicate well in marriage?

4. One common communication barrier in marriage is differing styles of communication. What are some common differences between the ways men and women communicate? between the ways introverted and outgoing individuals communicate?

5. Another common barrier to communication for most couples is the pressure of a busy lifestyle. How does this kind of pressure sometimes make it difficult to communicate with each other?

6. We all learn about how to communicate—and how *not* to communicate—by observing the behavior of others. The most enduring lessons in communication usually come from our parents. What did your parents do *well* in communicating with each other? What did they *not* do well? (Be specific.) If you were not raised by both parents, focus on whomever raised you.

Answer questions 6 and 7 with your spouse. After answering, you may want to share an appropriate insight or discovery with the group.

7. What barriers to good communication have you adopted from your parents' example?

Communication Barriers and the Bible

8. Even Jesus experienced barriers to communication. Read Luke 10:38-42. What kept Martha from hearing Jesus' message? What was Jesus' solution to Martha's problem?

9. What are some ways to overcome the barriers we listed under question 3? Suggest at least one way to overcome each one.

10. Read Ephesians 4:14-16. What does this passage say about the connection between appropriate communication and spiritual maturity?

11. What do you think it means to speak "the truth in love"?

12. What is God's role in helping us overcome barriers to communication? What is our role in overcoming those barriers?

W R A P • U P   15   M I N U T E S

Stand facing your spouse, and think of something that
happened today that you'd like to tell your spouse
about. Before you start to speak, hold your open book
directly between you so that neither of you can see
the other's face. Take one minute to tell your spouse
about something that happened today, without moving
the book away. Then switch, and with the same barrier in place have your spouse take one minute to tell
you about something that happened today.

After the two minutes are up, sit back down, and talk
with the whole group about the following questions:

- How did it feel to have that barrier
  between you when you were trying to
  share with each other?

- How is that like the way barriers to communication hinder marriage relationships?

Close your session with
prayer, and make sure
couples Make a Date for
this session's
HomeBuilders Project
before they leave.

Make a Date

Make a date with your spouse to meet before the next session to complete the HomeBuilders Project. Your leader will ask at the next session for you to share one thing from this experience.

DATE

TIME

LOCATION

HOMEBUILDERS PROJECT　　　　　6 0　M I N U T E S

As a Couple [10 minutes]

Begin your sharing time by answering one or two of the following questions:

• What humorous thing (perhaps something you didn't want to mention in the group setting) has happened in your marriage as a result of miscommunication?

• What TV character would you compare yourself to when it comes to communication? Why?

• What do you like best about how your spouse communicates with you?

Individually [25 minutes]

1. What's one insight you've gained about communication within your marriage from this session?

2. What barriers do you and your spouse face in communication?

---

3. On the following continuums, carefully evaluate your own communication strengths and weaknesses by circling the number closest to where you would rank yourself. Think for a moment about each one before marking it.

	Never	Sometimes	Often

Verbally express love 1 2 3 4 5 6 7 8 9 10

Listen sincerely and
  attentively 1 2 3 4 5 6 7 8 9 10

Talk too much. 1 2 3 4 5 6 7 8 9 10

Talk through problems 1 2 3 4 5 6 7 8 9 10

Discuss situations logically . . . 1 2 3 4 5 6 7 8 9 10

Share intimately 1 2 3 4 5 6 7 8 9 10

Share goals and dreams 1 2 3 4 5 6 7 8 9 10

Give nonsexual touches
  in communication. 1 2 3 4 5 6 7 8 9 10

Provide encouragement 1 2 3 4 5 6 7 8 9 10

Address conflict
  appropriately 1 2 3 4 5 6 7 8 9 10

Avoid addressing conflict 1 2 3 4 5 6 7 8 9 10

Honestly express emotions. . . . 1 2 3 4 5 6 7 8 9 10

Interact as a Couple [25 minutes]

1. Share your answers with each other from the individual time. Lovingly discuss your perceptions of how accurately your spouse rated his or her communication strengths and weaknesses. *Note:* Resolve ahead of time that you will not argue!

2. How easy is it to face up to your own barriers to effective communication? Why?

3. In what ways do you complement each other in your strengths and weaknesses in communication?

4. What areas of improvement would you like to focus on during this HomeBuilders study? Choose no more than three to focus on during the next month.

5. What is one thing you can do during the next week to overcome a communication barrier?

6. Spend some time in prayer, confessing sin to God if needed. Ask him for guidance, wisdom, and power in improving your communication. Ask God to help you help each other overcome barriers to communication.

Remember to take your calendar to the next session for Make a Date.

Making Your Relationship a Priority

To develop positive communication patterns, you must make your marriage relationship a priority.

WARM • UP   15   MINUTES

A Modern Stone-Age Family

Read the following case study, and discuss thoughts that might fill in the blanks at the end.

Case Study

Wilma was getting fed up. Every night Fred came home from a hard day at the quarry and plopped in front of the TV to watch Championship Rock-Wrestling. He barely uttered a grunt the whole evening except for the noises he made while chowing down the brontosaurus ribs Wilma had prepared. Fred often ignored Pebbles and Dino, and he left Wilma to bear the brunt of the cavework and parenting chores. Wilma was so tired at night that she usually was asleep before Fred came to bed.

Finally Wilma was ready to explode, and one Saturday she confronted Fred.

Wilma says:

Fred responds:

Wilma counters:

Fred says:

After a few minutes of having fun with this scenario, discuss the following questions:

- What kinds of communication problems are Fred and Wilma experiencing?

- How have their priorities affected their communication? their relationship?

If a new couple has joined the group, be sure to pass books around to record names, phone numbers, and e-mail addresses.

- How could they improve their communication?

Project Report

Share one thing you learned from the HomeBuilders Project from last session.

BLUEPRINTS   60 MINUTES

A relationship is a living thing—it thrives with attention and withers when ignored. To maintain a healthy relationship, married couples should regularly examine how they spend their most precious resources—their time and energy— and determine whether they are following their

If you have a large group, form smaller groups of about six people to answer the Blueprints questions. Unless otherwise noted, answer the questions in your subgroup. After finishing each section, take time for subgroups to share their answers with the whole group.

priorities. Many couples find that each anniversary is a good time to evaluate priorities together.

Your Most Precious Resources

1. What pressures in your life make it a challenge for you to give your marriage the time and energy it needs to grow stronger?

2. How do the following passages relate to making your marriage and home a priority in your lives?

• Ephesians 5:15-16

• Philippians 2:1-4

• Song of Songs 7:10-13

3. What good examples of making a marriage relationship a priority have you seen modeled by other couples?

4. What effect would you say that priority has had on those couples' marriages?

5. What are some things you've done lately to make your relationship a priority?

Personalizing Your Marriage Priorities

6. How are you doing in making your marriage a priority?

Answer questions 6, 7, and 8 with your spouse. After answering, you may want to share an appropriate insight or discovery with the group.

7. What are some of the barriers you face as you think of taking time for your spouse every day?

8. As you look at your normal daily schedule, what could you change—what could you spend less time doing—to make more room for your relationship? What would be the best time of the day for you to set aside for time together?

Recreational Companionship

9. What have been some fun, creative dates you've had together since you were married? What type of effect have these had on your relationship?

10. What would it take for you to go out on dates—or on weekends together, away from the kids—more than you do?

Conserving Your Energy

11. What would happen if you were able to transfer the energy you normally give to your work to your family instead? What would that do to your family? What would that do to your work?

12. Understanding that transferring all of your energy from work to your family is likely impossible, what are some ways you *could* save more energy for your home life?

HomeBuilders Principle:
*For communication within a marriage to be effective,
you must reserve time and energy for your spouse.*

W R A P • U P   15   M I N U T E S

Wishing-Not Well

Dig out five coins. Any coins will do—but you may be
permanently giving up these coins. Form a circle if you
aren't already in one. Close your eyes, and listen as the
leader reads the following questions. Don't answer verbally, but for every question that you must answer
"yes," toss one coin into the center of the circle. Try
not to notice how others around you are responding.

- Within the last month, have you ever let your day
  get so full that you barely had time to say good
  morning and good night to your spouse?
- Have you recently ignored your spouse—even for
  a minute—because of something you were watch-
  ing on television?
- Within the last year, have you let work obliterate

a time together that the two of you had planned in advance?

- Within the last six months, have you let a dispute over children, friends, or activities come between you?
- Have you ever let a hobby or other interest consume so much of your time that your spouse felt neglected?

Now open your eyes, and look at all the coins in the center of your circle. Silently think about how each coin represents at least one dent in someone's marriage relationship. Consider what commitment you might want to make to God regarding making your marriage more of a priority in your life. If you feel comfortable doing so, share with the group any commitment you want to make. Then gather all the coins together, and have someone buy a treat (however small) for your next meeting.

Make a Date

Make a date with your spouse to meet before the next session to complete the HomeBuilders Project. Your leader will ask at the next session for you to share one thing from this experience.

DATE

_____

TIME

_____

LOCATION

HOMEBUILDERS PROJECT   6 o   M I N U T E S

As a Couple [10 minutes]

- Begin by sharing at least one example of a time you thought your spouse really made your marriage a priority.

- Tell your spouse about any commitment you made or considered making during the last session.

Individually [25 minutes]

1. What insight about communication in marriage have you gained from this session?

2. How do you feel about the amount of time and energy you are saving each day for your spouse? for your children?

3. How do you feel about the amount of time and energy your spouse saves each day for you? for your children?

4. What difference do you think receiving more of your spouse's time and energy would make in your life?

5. What could you do to make your marriage and your family a higher priority in your life? What will you do this week?

6. What differences do you think that change in priorities would make in your relationship and communication with your spouse?

Interact as a Couple [25 minutes]
1. Share your answers from previous questions.

2. If you haven't already chosen a time, what would be a good time each day for you to spend time talking together? You might want to start with just ten minutes, but set a time, and stick with it.

3. What changes would you need to make—and what obstacles would you need to overcome—to spend this time together?

4. Pray together, committing to God to follow through on making your marriage a higher priority this week.

Remember to take your calendar to the next session so you can Make a Date.

Communication 101

Learning to use basic communication skills will enhance understanding within your marriage.

W A R M • U P   15   M I N U T E S

At First Sight

Tell the group about one or two things that you saw in your spouse while you were dating that led you to begin thinking, "This is the person I want to marry."

Project Report

Share one thing you learned from the HomeBuilders Project from last session.

If you have a large group, form smaller groups of about six people to answer the Blueprints questions. Unless otherwise noted, answer the questions in your subgroup. After finishing each section, take time for subgroups to share their answers with the whole group.

In this session you're going to take a look at the most basic part of pursuing understanding in your relationship—the components of communication. Words being uttered does not mean communication is taking place. For solid communication with understanding to happen, three components must be present: expressing, listening, and responding.

1. Read Proverbs 16:16 and 24:3. Why do you think "understanding" is important to a good marriage relationship?

The First Component: Expressing

When you say something to someone, you want that person to understand what you are saying and feeling. You want to be understood. So seek to express yourself clearly, and remember that you are using an incredibly powerful tool—the tongue.

2. Read James 3:3-12. According to this passage, what's dangerous about the tongue? Tell the group about a criticism or cruel comment that you remember from years ago. How did it affect you? (Note: Do *not* tell about something from your marriage!)

3. According to James 3:3-12, what's good about the tongue? Tell the group about an encouragement or compliment you received years ago that you've never forgotten. How did it affect you?

4. What's the danger in *not* expressing yourself openly and clearly?

Clear communication involves deliberate expression. To express yourself in a way that your spouse understands you, talk openly about what you *think*, what you *feel*, and what you *need* in the situation you are discussing.

The Second Component: Listening

When one person is talking, that person needs to be in the "spotlight." Each person needs a time of freedom for full expression without interruption or feedback. Unfortunately the person who is listening often wants to grab the spotlight, thus short-circuiting the communication process. When you have two or more people constantly fighting for the spotlight, caring only about expressing themselves, communication completely breaks down.

5. Take turns with your spouse being in the "spotlight." When it's your turn, spend about five minutes talking to your spouse about a problem you currently are experiencing *outside of your marriage relationship*. The problem could be at work, at home with a child, with a neighbor, or with a family member. Tell your spouse what you think and feel about the situation, and what you need from him or her. For this exercise in your group, don't direct any criticism toward your spouse. And when it's not your turn to be in the spotlight, keep quiet! Don't interrupt your mate!

For Extra Impact: Gather enough flashlights so that each couple can have one. Lower the lights in the meeting room, and have one spouse shine the "spotlight" on the other (without shining it in anyone's eyes!) while it's his or her turn to talk.

After both of you have been in the "spotlight," discuss questions 6-8 within your group.

6. How did you feel when you were the one talking for five minutes? How did you feel as you were listening?

7. Read James 1:19. Why do you think it is good to be "quick to listen" and "slow to speak"? What makes being a good listener so difficult?

8. Think of two or three good listeners you know. How do you feel about spending time with them? Why do you think that's so?

Listening isn't always easy to do. Often we want to jump in and give advice or fix someone's problem. However, listening carefully is a key to understanding your spouse's true needs.

The Third Component: Responding

At some point in almost every conversation, you need to move beyond listening. You need to join the conversation and seek to truly understand what your spouse is saying. You can do that by responding with appropriate feedback.

9. What kinds of inappropriate responses do we sometimes give that don't promote better understanding?

10. What are some appropriate types of feedback that work toward better understanding? How does appropriate feedback help build an environment of openness and trust in your communication?

One thing your spouse needs to know is that you are committed to him or her. You want to make the relationship work. You want to listen, and you want to help. One simple feedback question will communicate this desire if stated sincerely:

"What do you need most from me right now?"

At times your spouse will ask you to suggest a solution to a problem. At other times he or she may just need you to listen. Your responsibility is to be sincerely interested and ready to respond with what your spouse needs.

11. Read John 14:16-17. What other resource do you have for helping you build understanding within your marriage?

The three components to basic communication—expressing, listening, and giving appropriate feedback—may sound simple, but mastering them is a lifelong challenge! Like any new skill, they require lots of practice. But the important thing is that you get started and keep at it. Your first few tries at changing your communication patterns may be less than perfect, but keep trying. The eventual results will be well worth any initial difficulties.

HomeBuilders Principle:
You can foster positive communication in your marriage by using basic communication skills—expressing, listening, and responding.

Read the following situations. After each one, brain-storm appropriate initial responses for the spouse in the situation to give. Remember that responses can be questions. List suggested responses that seem especially appropriate to you.

- Janice can tell there's something wrong the minute Jim comes home from work. At first Jim refuses to talk about it, but finally blurts out, "I think I'm going to lose my job. It's not my fault, but I'm pretty sure it's going to happen. I don't know what we're going to do!"

- Mark gets annoyed that Susan spends so much of each weekend cleaning the house when he doesn't think it looks that bad. Susan gets annoyed that all Mark wants to do on the weekends is watch sports. One Saturday Susan steps in front of the football game on TV and turns it off. She turns to Mark and says, "We've got to talk! I'm sick of doing all the work around here while all you do is watch TV! I don't think this marriage is working."

After brainstorming good responses, look at what you've listed, and determine to use this kind of feedback in communication with your spouse.

Make a Date

Make a date with your spouse to meet before the next session to complete the HomeBuilders Project. Your leader will ask at the next session for you to share one thing from this experience.

DATE

TIME

LOCATION

As a Couple [10 minutes]

- Tell your spouse about something he or she has done for you that you really appreciated.
- Tell your spouse about something he or she has said to you that you really appreciated.

Individually [20 minutes]

1. What were your most significant insights from this week's session?

2. How would you rate yourself on a scale of one (poor) to five (excellent) as a clear communicator? as a sincere listener? as an appropriate responder?

3. How would you rate your spouse on a scale of one (poor) to five (excellent) as a clear communicator? as a sincere listener? as an appropriate responder?

4. What do you appreciate about the conversation skills of your spouse?

5. What do you need to work on most in improving your communication skills?

6. What's one concern in your marriage that you'd like to discuss with your spouse before this date is over?

Interact as a Couple [30 minutes]

1. Go over the first five questions in the previous section. Be open, kind, and understanding as you address difficult issues.

2. Tell each other about the concerns you listed under question 6. Tackle those concerns one at a time, following the components of communication learned in this week's session. Be sure to speak, listen, and respond only at the appropriate times. Follow the steps even if it feels awkward—it will become more natural with practice. When it's your time to give feedback, ask questions to help clarify your understanding. Summarize what you think you've heard, and ask if you understood correctly. Before you leave each concern, be sure to ask, "What do you need most from me right now?"

3. Wrap up your time together with prayer, committing to practice good communication skills within your marriage in the coming weeks.

Remember to take your calendar to the next session so you can Make a Date.

"Closing the Loop" in Conflict

Resolving conflict requires taking the initiative to mend the relationship.

W A R M • U P   15   M I N U T E S

Minor Irritations

Conflict is inevitable when two people live together. In his book *Staying Close*, Dennis Rainey lists a number of seemingly small things that often can spark arguments and conflicts. Tell the group about one of these that has caused a now-humorous conflict in your marriage. Or tell about a different one that stands out in your mind.

- Sleeping in the dark or with a night light on
- Leaving windows open or closed
- Where to keep the house temperature
- How to eat food

- How to blow your nose
- What kind of music to play on the stereo
- How loud the music is played
- Where clothing is thrown after it's taken off
- The proper way to hang toilet paper
- What time to go to bed or get up
- Whether the cap is kept on the toothpaste tube
- Whether cupboard doors are closed
- Who makes the bed, and how
- Who locks the door at night

Project Report

Share one thing you learned from the HomeBuilders Project from last session.

BLUEPRINTS   60 MINUTES

When you put two people together in marriage, conflict is inevitable. The differences between men and women alone ensure many rounds of arguments.
On top of that, any two people come from different

backgrounds, enjoy different hobbies and interests, and relate to people in different ways.

If you have a large group, form smaller groups of about six people to answer the Blueprints questions. Unless otherwise noted, answer the questions in your subgroup. After finishing each section, take time for subgroups to share their answers with the whole group.

Many couples manage to ignore these differences during courtship and engagement. But sometime after the honeymoon glow wears off, they begin experiencing conflict and may realize they tend to deal with that friction in opposite ways.

1. Why do you think so many couples do poorly at resolving the conflict they inevitably face in marriage?

God delights in restoring broken relationships. In seeking to help couples rebuild relationships, a common sequence of events has appeared in most conflicts. Each time a conflict begins, a loop is formed, and that loop is closed only when the conflict is resolved. "Closing the Loop" is what we want to see happen. More information on this concept can be found in *Dr. Rosberg's Do-It-Yourself Relationship Mender* (Tyndale House Publishing).

The Loop Opens

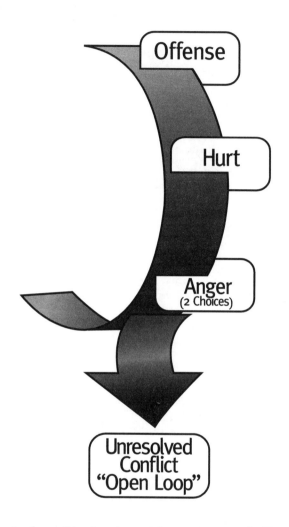

A typical conflict begins with some type of offense—one person does something to offend his or her spouse. The spouse is usually hurt by the offense, and that hurt often quickly gives way to anger.

Quiche Again?

Case Study

Sue works about six hours a day, while the couple's three children are in school. She arrives home on a typical afternoon at 3:30, and then heads out to take the children to basketball practice and piano lessons. She arrives back home at 5:30, just before her husband, Brian, returns home from his own day at work.

Brian finds Sue in the kitchen, starting dinner for the family. He sniffs the air and says, "Having quiche *again*? I'm getting tired of that stuff. Can't you come up with anything else?"

"Hey, I don't see you at work in the kitchen, do I?" Sue retorts angrily. "I'm tired of you complaining about my cooking. I'd be glad to have you take over the cooking anytime you want!"

2. Put yourself in Sue's shoes: How do you think she feels when she hears Brian's comment?

3. How does anger affect a person's response in a conflict?

The Fork in the Road

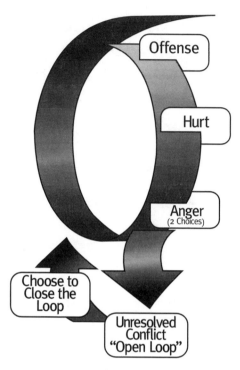

Offense

Hurt

Anger
(2 Choices)

Choose to
Close the
Loop

Unresolved
Conflict
"Open Loop"

At this point in a conflict, you come to a critical fork in the relationship road: This is where you need to decide if you will resolve the conflict or let it pass. Do you close the loop or leave it open?

4. What might keep Brian and Sue from taking the initiative to resolve their conflict?

5. What happens in a marriage relationship when conflicts are left unresolved?

6. What do the following verses say about closing the loop and resolving conflict?

Matthew 18:21-22

Ephesians 4:26-27

7. Give an example from your marriage—or from the marriage of someone you know—of what happens in a relationship when a "loop" is left open and conflict is not resolved. Don't share anything that would embarrass or irritate your spouse or anyone else.

> **HomeBuilders Principle:**
> *You should seek to resolve conflict so that your marriage relationship is not damaged.*

Closing the Loop

Step One: Preparing Your Heart

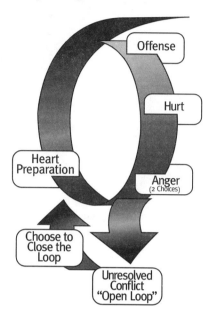

8. What guidance can you draw from the following passages for preparing your heart to resolve a conflict?

Psalm 139:23-24

1 Peter 3:8-9

> **HomeBuilders Principle:**
> *Resolving conflict is possible only when both of you
> are willing to humble yourselves.*

Step Two: Loving Confrontation

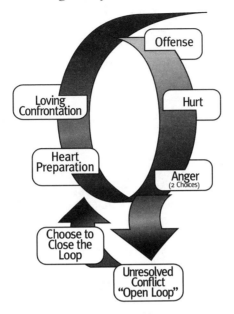

In this step, you discuss the conflict with your spouse. It's important to use the components of good communication we discussed in the last session. For example, focus on listening to your spouse rather than doing all the talking yourself. Also, be sure to choose the right time and place to discuss the conflict.

Answer the following two questions with your spouse. After answering, you may want to share an appropriate insight or discovery with the group.

9. In your relationship, why are certain times better than others for working through a conflict?

10. Read Proverbs 12:18. How have your spouse's "reckless words" pierced you? How have you used such words to pierce your spouse? How can a wise tongue bring healing to your relationship?

> **HomeBuilders Principle:**
> *Confrontation is usually necessary to resolve conflict, but you must do it lovingly.*

Step Three: Seeking Forgiveness

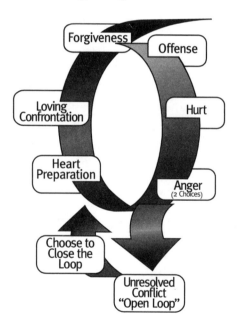

Forgiveness is vital in closing the loop in a relationship. Without it, you're trapped by anger; you'll never know the reconciliation of two hearts that once again are tender toward each other. Forgiveness includes four components: confession (I am wrong), sorrow (I am sorry), repentance (I don't want to hurt you again), and the request (will you forgive me?).

11. Read Ephesians 4:32. What does it mean to forgive others just as in Christ God forgave you? Why is it so difficult to do?

> **HomeBuilders Principle:**
> *Forgiveness is the key element in resolving conflict.*

Step Four: Regaining Trust

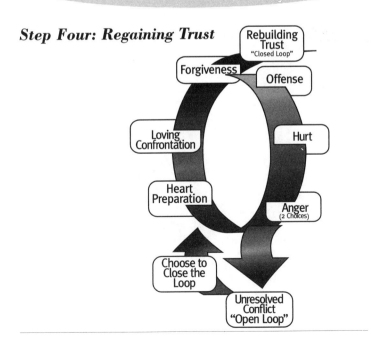

More Quiche?

Case Study Follow-up

After a loving confrontation, Brian realizes he's been too hard on Sue about cooking meals when she's as busy as he is. He asks for her forgiveness and promises to help out more at dinnertime—and not to complain about what Sue fixes.

12. If you were Sue, would you now trust Brian to quit complaining and handle his part of preparing dinner? Why or why not? What must Brian do to regain Sue's trust?

HomeBuilders Principle:
Forgiving your spouse does not always mean that you will automatically trust him or her; trust must be earned.

W R A P • U P   15 M I N U T E S

Read the following conflict situation:

During eight years of marriage, Sheila has repeatedly mishandled her family's finances. She has not kept a good accounting of what was in the checking account, and she has spent freely. As a result, she and her husband, Darrin, have a growing debt and a bad credit record. They just had a new-car loan denied, and Darrin is very angry.

Walk through each of the steps presented in this session, suggesting what could be said and done at each step to "close the loop."

- Step One: Preparing Your Heart

- Step Two: Loving Confrontation

- Step Three: Seeking Forgiveness

- Step Four: Regaining Trust

Share with the group the most important thing you've learned from this session about handling conflict.

Make a Date

Make a date with your spouse to meet before the next session to complete the HomeBuilders Project. Your leader will ask at the next session for you to share one thing from this experience.

DATE

TIME

LOCATION

HOMEBUILDERS PROJECT   6 0   M I N U T E S

As a Couple [10 minutes]

Answer the following three questions together, trying to agree on your answer:

• Which one of you is the better board-game player?

• Which one of you is funnier?

• Which one of you is sexier?

Individually [20 minutes]

1. Review the material from the Blueprints section. What are some of the main things you learned during the session?

2. Do you ever find yourself getting stuck at a certain stage in the conflict-resolution process? Why?

3. What do you personally need to work on in your conflict-resolution skills?

4. What is a conflict you have faced in your marriage relationship during the past month? Is there an open loop that needs to be closed?

5. At what stage in the "Closing the Loop" sequence do you currently find yourselves in this conflict?

6. What do you (not your spouse) need to do to work toward resolution? Have you come to the point of forgiveness?

Interact as a Couple [30 minutes]
1. Go through the first three questions that you answered individually, and share your answers.

2. Now work through questions 4-6, approaching each conflict separately. Begin by praying together, asking God to give you humility, insight, and wisdom as you discuss the conflict and how you can resolve it. Remember to follow the steps to closing the loop on conflict.

Remember to bring your calendar to the next session so you can Make a Date.

Communicating Through the Trials of Life

God can use you to encourage your spouse during times of trial.

WARM • UP   15 MINUTES

Typical Trials

Discuss the following question for each of the events that follow.

What are typical struggles or trials a couple faces when...

- they're newly married?
- they've had their first baby?
- they try to figure out and live by a budget?
- they move a thousand miles from "home"?
- there's a teenager in the house?
- old-age sets in?

Project Report

Share one thing you learned from the HomeBuilders Project from last session.

BLUEPRINTS   60 MINUTES

Anticipating the Trials

In June 1995, an American F-16 fighter jet was shot down in enemy terrain over northern Bosnia. Six days later, its pilot, Scott O'Grady, was rescued by a Marine helicopter team. Americans were fascinated by O'Grady's story—how he ate insects, captured rain water to ease his thirst, and narrowly evaded Bosnian search teams.

O'Grady's survival was a testament to his Air Force training. He had completed a seventeen-day survival school where he learned to live off the land and to maintain a positive mental attitude. When he left on his mission, he wore a survival vest packed with equipment. Even his seat, which ejected with him, contained invaluable equipment. O'Grady was prepared for his ordeal.

He knew what to do when the trials came. Trials are an inevitable part of life. Scott O'Grady was able to handle six days on his own in hostile territory. Yet few people are prepared to handle the unavoidable storms of life.

If you have a large group, form smaller groups of about six to answer the Blueprints questions. Unless otherwise noted, answer the questions in your subgroup. After finishing each section, take time for subgroups to share their answers with the whole group.

1. Read James 1:2-4. Note that James talks about "whenever" trials come and not "if." Why is it that few of us are well prepared to handle trials and suffering?

2. What typically happens in a marriage relationship when trials occur?

3. How has your marriage relationship been affected by trials and stresses you've faced?

HomeBuilders Principle:
As a couple, you must be prepared for the trials that will inevitably occur during your life together.

Preparing for the Trials

Respond to 4 and 5 with your spouse. When you're done, you may want to share an appropriate insight or discovery with the group.

4. Look ahead to the next twenty to thirty years of your marriage. List the trials and stresses you likely will face at some point (some examples: death of parents, adjustments to in-laws, putting kids through college):

•

•

•

•

•

•

5. How do you expect these trials to affect your relationship?

Turning to God in the Trials of Life

6. Form three groups and have each group look at one of the following passages to answer this question: What does this passage say about *why* God allows trials and suffering? After a few minutes, report to the entire group what your small group discovered.

Romans 8:28

1 Peter 1:3-9

1 Peter 4:12-14

7. What is something good that came out of a trial you faced?

8. Read the following passages. What do these passages say about how God relates to us during times of stress or trial?

1 Corinthians 10:13

2 Corinthians 1:3-4

Philippians 4:12-13

9. How have you seen the truth of one of these Scriptures in your life?

10. Read Philippians 4:4-7. What does this passage say about *how* we're to face the trials of our lives? What makes this difficult? How can we exhibit the attitudes and actions described in this passage?

Communicating in the Trials of Life

11. Read Ecclesiastes 4:9-10. How would you apply this passage to your marriage relationship? Tell about a time you saw this principle at work in your marriage.

W R A P • U P   15   M I N U T E S

Some people tend to pull away from their mates during difficult times. But God intends that spouses support each other in times of trial. Every couple needs to make a conscious commitment to work through trials together.

Once you've made that commitment, the following four principles will help you communicate during trials in such a way that you build up each other. These principles can revolutionize your marriage if you practice them. Read each principle and answer the question following it with your spouse.

1. *Determine what you need from each other.* The easiest way to learn this is just to ask each other, "What do you need from me right now?" on a regular basis. We call this "taking our temperature."

- Ask your spouse, "What do you need from me right now?"

2. *Determine to face the problem head-on together.* Often we hope the pain will go away if we focus our attention on other things or if we fill our hours with activities. It won't work—the pain must be faced.

- What problem do you need to face head-on together?

3. *Point each other to God.* Pray together as a couple. Read Scripture to each other. (Psalms 23, 31, and 34 are a few good selections.) Maintain your relationship to God as his children, and help your spouse do the same.

- Pray together with your spouse about a trial you're facing.

4. *Seek help from friends and family.* As a couple you may be tempted to isolate yourself from your children, friends, and family in a time of trial. Instead, you need to admit your need and your helplessness, and allow the body of Christ to fulfill its function in supporting you.

- Who do you need to turn to for help with a trial you're facing?

Share with the whole group any insights you've gained from these principles. What are some problems you are facing right now? How can this group pray for you?

HomeBuilders Principle:
You and your spouse can help each other persevere and even experience joy during trials by encouraging each other and by pointing each other to God.

Make a Date

Make a date with your spouse to meet before the next session to complete the HomeBuilders Project. Your leader will ask at the next session for you to share one thing from this experience.

DATE

TIME

LOCATION

HOMEBUILDERS PROJECT   6 0   M I N U T E S

As a Couple [10 minutes]
Recall a trial you've faced as a couple that you can look back and smile about. Share with each other what you gained and learned from that trial.

Individually [20 minutes]
1. Look over your notes from the session and write down the key insights you gained.

2. As you look back on your marriage, how would you evaluate your success at dealing with the trials you've faced so far? What have been the reasons for your success or lack of success?

3. What trials are you facing right now that you need to deal with? How can your spouse help you? How can God help you?

4. Look back at Blueprints questions 4 and 5 of this session. How prepared do you feel for the trials you will face during the next twenty to thirty years? How can you prepare together for facing those upcoming trials?

5. How fully do you lean on God and your spouse during times of stress and suffering? What can you do to improve?

Interact as a Couple [30 minutes]

1. Share your responses to the questions you answered individually.

2. Decide on and commit to three ways you'll begin applying the principles of this session to your lives during the next week. Gently hold each other accountable for following through on your commitments.

3. Close your time in prayer. If you are going through trials right now, use the verses from the Blueprints section to guide you in prayer. Ask God to give you joy during these trials, and pray that you will be an encouragement to each other.

Remember to bring your calendar to the next session so you can Make a Date.

Achieving Spiritual Intimacy

The best and deepest level of communication is
achieved when you seek God together.

W A R M • U P   15   M I N U T E S

Moving Forward

Spread out as much as possible in your meeting area,
but stay with your spouse. Stand side by side with
your spouse, facing the same direction, and move
about three feet apart. Place one of your books on the
floor several steps out in front of you. Then listen as
your leader reads the following descriptive statements. After each statement, take one small step
toward your book. It doesn't matter if you do what the
statement describes, take a step after each one.

• You maintain a regular personal quiet time and
  share insights with your spouse.

- You share together how that week's sermon affected you.
- You pray together.
- You have devotions together.
- You apply the Bible's principles to your personal life and marriage.
- You seek God's will in your decisions.

Discuss the following questions in your group:

- What happened to the distance between you and your spouse as you moved toward your book?
- How is this like what happens when you seek to draw closer to God in your lives and marriages?
- How would doing what the statements said make a difference in communication within your marriage?

Project Report

Share one thing you learned from the HomeBuilders Project from last session.

BLUEPRINTS 60 MINUTES

Many of the principles we've discussed for better

ROUTE ITEM

Title:	Improving communication in your marriage / by Gary and Barbara Rosberg.
Author:	Rosberg, Gary, 1952-
Call Number:	268.6407 R789
Enumeration:	
Chronology:	
Copy:	1
Item Barcode:	*34711001764564*
Route To:	LCC CIRCULATION

communication within marriages could be applied just as well by non-Christians. You don't have to be a believer in Jesus Christ to make time in your schedule for your spouse, to save energy for when you get home, or to "close the loop" in conflicts. But a truly Christian marriage will be different from any other.

If you have a large group, form smaller groups of about six to answer the Blueprints questions. Unless otherwise noted, answer the questions in your subgroup. After finishing each section, take time for subgroups to share their answers with the whole group.

1. What do you think should make a Christian marriage—and communication within that marriage—distinctive?

The Best Part of Marriage

Spiritual intimacy is one ingredient of marriage that is available only to those who have a personal relationship with God through Jesus Christ and live their lives seeking to please him. When a husband and wife are both growing in their vertical relationships with God, the horizontal relationship between them tends to come together as well. This is the best part of marriage!

2. Read Acts 4:31-32. How did the Christians begin to relate to one another after they had been filled with the Holy Spirit? What do you think it means to be "one in heart and mind" in a marriage relationship?

3. Why is it that even Christian couples are sometimes critical and selfish toward each other?

4. Read Colossians 3:12-17. How would it affect your marriage relationship if you as "God's chosen people" let the "peace of Christ rule in your hearts"?

5. What kinds of actions and experiences will lead toward achieving deeper spiritual intimacy with your spouse?

HomeBuilders Principle:
Truly intimate communication comes only when you seek God as a couple and let him knit your hearts together.

Taking Action

Many Christian couples wish they spent more time together praying and reading the Word of God. They know what they should do, but they don't do it. A typical comment is, "I know we should have more of a spiritual life together, and I want that, but we just don't ever seem to get around to doing anything about it."

Some couples have simply never built into their lives the discipline of spending time together with God. If you've been faithful in completing the HomeBuilders Projects in this study, however, you have a good start! You've actually begun to create a new discipline in your lives.

6. Why is it so difficult to make your spiritual lives together a priority?

7. If you were to pray together and study the Bible together more consistently, how do you think it would affect your marriage? What are some practical ways to pray and study the Bible together as a couple?

8. Read James 1:22-25. How does this passage relate to our taking action on what we know God wants us to do in our marriages?

Answer questions 9-11 with your spouse. After answering, you may want to share an appropriate insight or discovery with the group.

9. How has your spiritual intimacy improved as you've completed the HomeBuilders projects?

10. What can you do to continue this new discipline in your lives? Choose one step right now that you'll commit to taking. What kinds of resources will you need? When will you take action?

11. What types of things are likely to get in the way of your continuing this discipline? What can you do to keep your commitment from falling by the wayside?

For Extra Impact

If you have time during this session, begin working together as a couple on the Bible study given in this session's HomeBuilders Project. Even if you complete only one question, this experience will help you see the kinds of things you can learn and gain by studying the Bible together.

HomeBuilders Principle:
You can grow spiritual intimacy in your marriage by regularly praying and studying the Bible together.

W R A P • U P   15   M I N U T E S

As you come to the end of this study, reflect as a group on what you have experienced. Pick one of the following questions to answer and share with the group.

• What has this group meant to you during the course of this study? Be specific.

• What is the most valuable thing you discovered?

- What would you like to see happen next for this group?

- How have you changed as a result of what you've learned in this study?

Make a Date

Make a date with your spouse to meet this week to do the HomeBuilders Project Bible study together.

_____
DATE

_____
TIME

_____
LOCATION

As a Couple [30-60 minutes]

Complete the following Bible study this week.
Continue your habit of taking one evening a week to
study the Bible together, just as you've worked on the
HomeBuilders Projects during this course. If you
need help finding a resource for further Bible study
as a couple, talk to your group leader or your pastor.

Bible Study: 1 Corinthians 13

Read the Scripture passages together and then answer
the questions. Talk about what you can do in your
day-to-day relationship to strengthen your marriage
and family through what you learn from God's Word.
Pray together that God will help you follow through
on strengthening your marriage.

1. 1 Corinthians 13 is often referred to as the love
chapter. As you read it, how do you feel when you read
the different descriptions of love? How well have you

fulfilled them in your relationship with your spouse?

2. How would you contrast the different messages about love from our culture with the message of this passage?

3. What impresses you most about this passage? Which of these principles have you seen embodied in your spouse in some way?

4. Verse 8 tells us, "love never fails." What do you need to do in your marriage to strengthen the never-fail love that God wants to thrive in your marriage?

5. Look through all the descriptions of love. In what area do you most need to change to exercise God-honoring love to your spouse?

Please visit our Web site at www.familylife.com/homebuilders
to give us your feedback on this study and to get information
on other FamilyLife resources and conferences.

Where Do You Go From Here?

It is our prayer that you have benefited greatly from this study in the HomeBuilders Couples Series. We hope that your marriage will continue to grow as you both submit your lives to Jesus Christ and build according to his blueprints.

We also hope that you will begin reaching out to strengthen other marriages in your community and local church. Your church needs couples like you who are committed to building Christian marriages. A favorite World War II story illustrates this point very clearly.

The year was 1940. The French Army had just collapsed under Hitler's onslaught. The Dutch had folded, overwhelmed by the Nazi regime. The Belgians had surrendered. And the British Army was trapped on the coast of France in the channel port of Dunkirk.

Two hundred and twenty thousand of Britain's finest young men seemed doomed to die, turning the English Channel red with their blood. The Fuehrer's troops, only miles away in the hills of France, didn't realize how close to victory they actually were.

Any rescue seemed feeble and futile in the time remaining. A "thin" British Navy—"the professionals"—told King George VI that at best they could save 17,000 troops. The House of Commons was warned to prepare for "hard and heavy tidings."

Politicians were paralyzed. The king was powerless. And the Allies could only watch as spectators from a distance. Then as the doom of the British Army seemed imminent, a strange fleet appeared on the horizon of the English Channel—the wildest assortment of boats perhaps ever assembled in history. Trawlers, tugs, scows, fishing sloops, lifeboats, pleasure craft, smacks and coasters, sailboats, even the London fire-brigade flotilla. *Each ship was manned by civilian volunteers—English fathers sailing to rescue Britain's exhausted, bleeding sons.*

William Manchester writes in his epic novel, *The Last Lion*, that even today what happened in 1940 in less than twenty-four hours seems like a miracle—not only were all of the British soldiers rescued, but 118,000 other Allied troops as well.

Today the Christian home is much like those troops at Dunkirk. Pressured, trapped, and demoralized, it needs help. Your help. The Christian community may be much like England—we stand waiting for politicians, professionals, even for our pastors to step in and save the family. But the problem is much larger than all of those combined can solve.

With the highest divorce rate of any nation on earth, we need an all-out effort by men and women "sailing" to rescue the exhausted and wounded family casualties. We need an outreach effort by common couples with faith in an uncommon God. For too long, married couples within the church have abdicated the privilege and responsibility of influencing others to those in full-time vocational ministry.

Possibly this study has indeed been used to "light the torch" of your spiritual lives. Perhaps it was already burning, and this provided more fuel. Regardless, may we challenge you to invest your lives in others?

You and other couples around the world can team together to build thousands of marriages and families. By starting a HomeBuilders group, you will not only strengthen other marriages; you will also see your marriage grow as you share these principles with others.

Will You Join Us in "Touching Lives...Changing Families"?

The following are some practical ways you can make a difference in families today:

1. Gather a group of four to seven couples, and lead them through the six sessions of this HomeBuilders study, *Improving Communication in Your Marriage*. (Why not consider challenging others in your church or community to form additional HomeBuilders groups?)

2. Commit to continue marriage building by doing another course in the HomeBuilders Couples Series.

3. An excellent outreach tool is the film *"JESUS,"* which is available on video. For more information, contact FamilyLife at 1-800-FL-TODAY.

4. Host a dinner party. Invite families from your neighborhood to your home, and as a couple share your faith in Christ.

5. Reach out and share the love of Christ with neighborhood children.

6. If you have attended the FamilyLife Marriage Conference, why not offer to assist your pastor in counseling couples engaged to be married, using the material you received?

For more information about any of the above ministry opportunities, contact your local church, or write:

> **FamilyLife**
> P.O. Box 8220
> Little Rock, AR 72221-8220
> 1-800-FL-TODAY
> **www.familylife.com**

Our Problems, God's Answers

•

Every couple eventually has to deal with problems in marriage.Communication problems. Money problems. Difficulties with sexual intimacy. These issues are important to cultivating a strong, loving relationship with your spouse. The HomeBuilders Couples Series is designed to help you strengthen your marriage in many of these critical areas.

Part One: The Big Problem

One basic problem is at the heart of every other problem in every marriage, and it's a problem we can't help you fix. No matter how hard you try, this is one problem that is too big for you to deal with on your own.

The problem is separation from God. If you want to experience marriage the way it was designed to be, you need a vital relationship with the God who created you and offers you the power to live a life of joy and purpose.

And what separates us from God is one more problem—sin. Most of us have assumed throughout our lives that the term "sin" refers to a list of bad habits that everyone agrees are wrong. We try to deal with our sin problem by working hard to become better people. We read books to learn how to control our anger, or we resolve to stop cheating on our taxes.

But in our hearts, we know our sin problem runs much deeper than a list of bad habits. All of us have rebelled against God. We have ignored him and have decided to run our own lives in a way that makes sense to us. The Bible says that the God who created us wants us to follow his plan for our lives. But because of our sin problem, we think our ideas and plans are better than his.

- *"For all have sinned and fall short of the glory of God"* (Romans 3:23).

What does it mean to "fall short of the glory of God"? It means that none of us has trusted and treasured God the way we should. We have sought to satisfy ourselves with other things and have treated those things as more valuable than God. We have gone our own way. According to the Bible, we have to pay a penalty for our sin. We cannot simply do things the way we choose and hope it will all be OK with God. Following our own plan leads to our destruction.

- *"There is a way that seems right to a man, but in the end it leads to death"* (Proverbs 14:12).
- *"For the wages of sin is death"* (Romans 6:23a).

The penalty for sin is that we are forever separated from God's love. God is holy, and we are sinful. No matter how hard we try, we cannot come up with some plan, like living a good life or even trying to do what the Bible says, and hope that we can avoid the penalty.

God's Solution to Sin

Thankfully God has a way to solve our dilemma. He became a man through the person of Jesus Christ. He lived a holy life, in perfect obedience to God's plan. He also willingly died on a cross to pay our penalty for sin. Then he proved that he is more powerful than sin or death by rising from the dead. He alone has the power to overrule the penalty for our sin.

- *"Jesus answered, 'I am the way and the truth and the life. No one comes to the Father except through me' "* (John 14:6).

- *"But God demonstrates his own love for us in this: While we were still sinners, Christ died for us"* (Romans 5:8).

- *"Christ died for our sins...he was buried...he was raised on the third day according to the Scriptures...he appeared to Peter, and then to the Twelve. After that, he appeared to more than five hundred"* (1 Corinthians 15:3-6).

- *"For the wages of sin is death, but the gift of God is eternal life in Christ Jesus our Lord"* (Romans 6:23).

The death of Jesus has fixed our sin problem. He has bridged the gap between God and us. He is calling all of us to come to him and to give up our own flawed plan for how to run our lives. He wants us to trust God and his plan.

Accepting God's Solution

If you agree that you are separated from God, he is calling you to confess your sins. All of us have made messes of our lives because we have stubbornly preferred our ideas and plans over his. As a result, we deserve to be cut off from God's love and his care for us. But God has promised that if we will agree that we have rebelled against his plan for us and have messed up our lives, he will forgive us and will fix our sin problem.

- *"Yet to all who received him, to those who believed in his name, he gave the right to become children of God"* (John 1:12).

- *"For it is by grace you have been saved, through faith—and this not from yourselves, it is the gift of*

God—not by works, so that no one can boast" (Ephesians 2:8-9).

When the Bible talks about receiving Christ, it means we acknowledge that we are sinners and that we can't fix the problem ourselves. It means we turn away from our sin. And it means we trust Christ to forgive our sins and to make us the kind of people he wants us to be. It's not enough to just intellectually believe that Christ is the Son of God. We must trust in him and his plan for our lives by faith, as an act of the will.

Are things right between you and God, with him and his plan at the center of your life? Or is life spinning out of control as you seek to make your way on your own?

You can decide today to make a change. You can turn to Christ and allow him to transform your life. All you need to do is to talk to him and tell him what is stirring in your mind and in your heart. If you've never this before, considering taking the steps listed here:

- Do you agree that you need God? Tell God.

- Have you made a mess of your life by following your own plan? Tell God.

- Do you want God to forgive you? Tell God.

- Do you believe that Jesus' death on the cross and his resurrection from the dead gave him the power to fix your sin problem and to grant you the free gift of eternal life? Tell God.

- Are you ready to acknowledge that God's plan for your life is better than any plan you could come up with? Tell God.

- Do you agree that God has the right to be the Lord and master of your life? Tell God.

> *"Seek the Lord while he may be found;*
> *call on him while he is near"*
> (Isaiah 55:6).

Following is a suggested prayer:

> *Lord Jesus, I need you. Thank you for dying on the*
> *cross for my sins. I receive you as my Savior and Lord.*
> *Thank you for forgiving my sins and giving me eternal*
> *life. Make me the kind of person you want me to be.*

Does this prayer express the desire of your heart? If it does, pray it right now, and Christ will come into your life, as he promised.

Part Two: Living the Christian Life

For a person who is a follower of Christ—a Christian—the penalty for sin is paid in full. But the effect of sin continues throughout our lives.

- *"If we claim to be without sin, we deceive ourselves and the truth is not in us"* (1 John 1:8).

- *"For what I do is not the good I want to do; no, the evil I do not want to do—this I keep on doing"* (Romans 7:19).

The effects of sin carry over into our marriages as well. Even Christians struggle to maintain solid, God-honoring marriages. Most couples eventually realize that they can't do it on their own. But with God's help, they can succeed. The Holy Spirit can have a huge impact in the marriages of Christians who live constantly, moment by moment, under his gracious direction.

Self-Centered Christians

Many Christians struggle to live the Christian life in their own strength because they are not allowing God to control their lives. Their interests are self-directed, often resulting in failure and frustration.

- *"Brothers, I could not address you as spiritual but as worldly—mere infants in Christ. I gave you milk, not solid food, for you were not yet ready for it. Indeed, you are still not ready. You are still worldly. For since there is jealousy and quarreling among you, are you not worldly? Are you not acting like mere men?"* (1 Corinthians 3:1-3).

The self-centered Christian cannot experience the abundant and fruitful Christian life. Such people trust in their own efforts to live the Christian life: They are either uninformed about—or have forgotten—God's love, forgiveness, and power. This kind of Christian:

- has an up-and-down spiritual experience.

- cannot understand himself—he wants to do what is right, but cannot.

- fails to draw upon the power of the Holy Spirit to live the Christian life.

Some or all of the following traits may characterize the Christian who does not fully trust God:

Disobedience	Plagued by impure thoughts
Lack of love for God and others	Jealous
Inconsistent prayer life	Worrisome
Lack of desire for Bible study	Easily discouraged, frustrated
Legalistic attitude	Critical
	Lack of purpose

Note: The individual who professes to be a Christian but who continues to practice sin should realize that he may not be a Christian at all, according to 1 John 2:3; 3:6, 9; Ephesians 5:5.

Spirit-Centered Christians

When a Christian puts Christ on the throne of his life, he yields to God's control. This Christian's interests are directed by the Holy Spirit, resulting in harmony with God's plan.

- *"But the fruit of the Spirit is love, joy, peace, patience, kindness, goodness, faithfulness, gentleness and self-control. Against such things there is no law"* (Galatians 5:22-23).

Jesus said,

- *"I have come that they may have life, and have it to the full"* (John 10:10b).

- *"I am the vine; you are the branches. If a man remains in me and I in him, he will bear much fruit; apart from me you can do nothing"* (John 15:5).

- *"But you will receive power when the Holy Spirit comes on you; and you will be my witnesses in Jerusalem, and in all Judea and Samaria, and to the ends of the earth"* (Acts 1:8).

The following traits result naturally from the Holy Spirit's work in our lives:

Christ centered	Love
Holy Spirit empowered	Joy
Motivated to tell others about Jesus	Peace
	Patience
Dedicated to prayer	Kindness
Student of God's Word	Goodness
Trusts God	Faithfulness
Obeys God	Gentleness
	Self-control

The degree to which these traits appear in a Christian's life and marriage depends upon the extent to which the Christian trusts the Lord with every detail of life, and upon that person's maturity in Christ. One who is only beginning to understand the ministry of the Holy Spirit should not be discouraged if he is not as fruitful as mature Christians who have known and experienced this truth for a longer period of time.

Giving God Control

Jesus promises his followers an abundant and fruitful life as they allow themselves to be directed and empowered by the Holy Spirit. As we give God control of our lives, Christ lives in and through us in the power of the Holy Spirit (John 15).

If you sincerely desire to be directed and empowered by God, you can turn your life over to the control of the Holy Spirit right now (Matthew 5:6; John 7:37-39).

First, confess your sins to God, agreeing with him that you want to turn from any past sinful patterns in your life. Thank God in faith that he has forgiven all of your sins because Christ died for you (Colossians 2:13-15; 1 John 1:9; 2:1-3; Hebrews 10:1-18).

Be sure to offer every area of your life to God (Romans 12:1-2). Consider what areas you might rather keep to yourself, and be sure you're willing to give God control in those areas.

By faith, commit yourself to living according to the Holy Spirit's guidance and power.

- *Live by the Spirit: "So I say, live by the Spirit, and you will not gratify the desires of the sinful nature. For the sinful nature desires what is contrary to the Spirit, and the Spirit what is contrary to the sinful nature. They are in conflict with each other, so that you do not do what you want"* (Galatians 5:16-17).

- *Trust in God's Promise: "This is the confidence we have in approaching God: that if we ask anything according to his will, he hears us. And if we know that he hears us—whatever we ask—we know that we have what we asked of him"* (1 John 5:14-15).

Expressing Your Faith Through Prayer

Prayer is one way of expressing your faith to God. If the prayer that follows expresses your sincere desire, consider praying the prayer or putting the thoughts into your own words:

Dear God, I need you. I acknowledge that I have been directing my own life and that, as a result, I have sinned against you. I thank you that you have forgiven my sins through Christ's death on the cross for me. I now invite Christ to take his place on the throne of my life. Take control of my life through the Holy Spirit as you promised you would if I asked in faith. I now thank you for directing my life and for empowering me through the Holy Spirit.

Walking in the Spirit

If you become aware of an area of your life (an attitude or an action) that is displeasing to God, simply confess your sin, and thank God that he has forgiven your sins on the basis of Christ's death on the cross. Accept God's love and forgiveness by faith, and continue to have fellowship with him.

If you find that you've taken back control of your life through sin—a definite act of disobedience—try this exercise, "Spiritual Breathing," as you give that control back to God.

1. Exhale. Confess your sin. Agree with God that you've sinned against him, and thank him for his forgiveness of it, according to 1 John 1:9 and Hebrews 10:1-25. Remember that confession involves repentance, a determination to change attitudes and actions.

2. Inhale. Surrender control of your life to Christ, inviting the Holy Spirit to once again take charge. Trust that he now directs and empowers you, according to the command of Galatians 5:16, 17 and the promise of 1 John 5:14, 15. Returning to your faith in God enables you to continue to experience God's love and forgiveness.

Revolutionizing Your Marriage

This new commitment of your life to God will enrich your marriage. Sharing with your spouse what you've committed to is a powerful step in solidifying your own commitment. As you exhibit the Holy Spirit's work within you, your spouse may be drawn to make the same commitment you've made. If both of you have given control of your life to the Holy Spirit, you'll be able to help each other remain true to God, and your marriage may be revolutionized. With God in charge of your lives, life becomes an amazing adventure.

Leader's Notes

Contents

About Leading a HomeBuilders Group

What is the leader's job?

Your role is that of "facilitator"—one who encourages people to think and to discover what Scripture says, who helps group members feel comfortable, and who keeps things moving forward.

What is the best setting and time schedule for this study?

This study is designed as a small group home Bible study. However, it can be adapted for use in a Sunday school setting as well. Here are some suggestions for using this study in a small group and in a Sunday school class:

In a small group

To create a friendly and comfortable atmosphere, it is recommended that you do this study in a home setting. In many cases the couple that leads the study also serves as host to the group. Sometimes involving another couple as host is a good idea. Choose the option you believe will work best for your group, taking into account factors such as the number of couples participating and the location.

Each session is designed as a ninety-minute study; but we recommend a two-hour block of time. This will allow you to move through each part of the study at a more relaxed pace. However, be sure to keep in mind one of the cardinal rules of a small group: Good groups start *and* end on time. People's time is valuable, and your group will appreciate you being respectful of this.

In a Sunday school class

There are two important adaptations you need to make if you want to use this study in a class setting: 1) The material you cover should focus on the content from the Blueprints section of each session. Blueprints is the heart of each session and is designed to last sixty minutes. 2) Most Sunday school classes are taught in a teacher format instead of a small group format. If this study will be used in a class setting, the class should adapt to a small group dynamic. This will involve an interactive, discussion-based format and may also require a class to break into multiple smaller groups (we recommend groups of six to eight people).

What is the best size group?

We recommend from four to eight couples (including you and your spouse). If you have more people interested than you think you can accommodate, consider asking someone else to lead a second group. If you have a large group, you are encouraged at various times in the study to break into smaller subgroups. This helps you cover the material in a timely fashion and allows for optimum interaction and participation within the group.

What about refreshments?

Many groups choose to serve refreshments, which help create an environment of fellowship. If you plan on including refreshments in your study, here are a couple of suggestions: 1) For the first session (or two) you should provide the refreshments and then allow the group to be involved by having people sign up to bring them on later dates.

2) Consider starting your group with a short time of informal fellowship and refreshments (fifteen minutes), then move into the study. If couples are late, they miss only the food and don't disrupt the study. You may also want to have refreshments available at the end of your meeting to encourage fellowship, but remember, respect the group members' time by ending the study on schedule and allowing anyone who needs to leave right away the opportunity to do so gracefully.

What about child care?

Groups handle this differently depending on their needs. Here are a couple of options you may want to consider:

- Have everyone be responsible for making their own arrangements.

- As a group, hire child care and have all the kids watched in one location.

What about prayer?

An important part of a small group is prayer. However, as the leader, you need to be sensitive to the level of comfort the people in your group have toward praying in front of others. Never call on people to pray aloud if you don't know if they are comfortable doing this. There are a number of creative approaches you can take, such as modeling prayer, calling for volunteers, and letting people state their prayers in the form of finishing a sentence. A tool that is helpful in a group is a prayer list. You are encouraged to do this, but let it be someone else's ministry to the group. You should lead the prayer time, but allow another couple in the group the opportunity to create, update, and distribute prayer lists.

In closing

An excellent resource that covers leading a HomeBuilders group in greater detail is the *HomeBuilders Leader Guide* by Drew and Kit Coons. This book may be obtained at your local Christian bookstore, or by contacting Group Publishing or FamilyLife.

About the
Leader's Notes

The sessions in this study can be easily led without a lot of preparation time. However, accompanying Leader's Notes have been provided to assist you in preparation. The categories within the Leader's Notes are as follows:

Objectives

The purpose of the Objectives is to help focus the issues that will be presented in each session.

Notes and Tips

This section will relate any general comments about the session. This information should be viewed as ideas, helps, and suggestions. You may want to create a checklist of things you want to be sure to do in each session.

Commentary

Included in this section are notes that relate specifically to Blueprints questions. Not all Blueprints questions in each session will have accompanying commentary notes. Questions with related commentaries are designated by numbers (e.g. Blueprints question 8 in Session One would correspond to number 8 in the Commentary section of Session One Leader's Notes).

Session One:
Understanding the Barriers to Communication

Objectives

Understanding the barriers to communication is the first step toward building strong communication necessary for a healthy marriage.

In this session, couples will...

• discuss why communication is so vital to a marriage.

• examine barriers to communication.

• look at some initial steps to overcoming those barriers.

Notes and Tips

1. If you have not already done so, you will want to read the information on pages 4 and 5 as well as "About Leading a HomeBuilders Group" and "About the Leader's Notes" starting on page 104.

2. As part of the first session you may want to review with the group some Ground Rules (see page 11 in the Introduction).

3. Because this is the first session, make a special point to tell the group about the importance of the HomeBuilders Project.

Encourage each couple to "Make a Date" for a time before the next meeting to complete the project. Mention that you will ask about this during Warm-Up of the next session.

4. This is the first session, so you may want to offer a closing prayer instead of asking others to pray aloud. Many people are uncomfortable praying in front of others, and unless you already know your group real well, it may be wise to slowly venture into various methods of prayer. Regardless of how you decide to close, you should serve as a model.

5. You may want to remind the group that because this group is just under way, it is not too late to invite another couple to join the group. Challenge everyone to think about couples they could invite to the next session.

6. The key in this week's study is to make each couple aware that it is OK to have barriers; we just need to determine what those barriers are and then develop a plan to overcome them. Couples are going to have some insecurities and may wonder, "Can I trust these people?" Remind the couples that you are a team and you are all working on sharpening your skills.

7. Consider using the following activity after question 4 in the Blueprints section as a way to help your group experience firsthand a typical barrier to communication. Before asking question 5, say, "Before we move on, I'm going to try a little experiment." Then either switch on a television or begin playing some music on a radio or cassette/CD player. Make

sure the television or music is loud enough to make conversation difficult, but don't turn it on so loud that you have to shout to be heard. Go ahead and discuss question 5 as normally as possible. Then ask, "Why do you think I made it so noisy in here? How does it make you feel when you're trying to talk to each other over that noise? How was the music a barrier to communication? How is that like what other barriers do in our communication?"

Commentary

Here is some additional information about various Blueprints questions. Note: The numbers below correspond to the Blueprints questions of the same numbers in the session. If you share any of these points, be sure to do so in a manner that does not stifle discussion by making you the authority with the real answers. Begin your comments by saying things like, "One thing I notice in this passage is…" or "I think another reason for this is…"

1. Many couples never receive training in how to communicate with each other. They may not have had good role models when they grew up, and they never learned communication skills. They don't understand the differences between themselves—or even the general differences between men and women. They feel a distance, and they don't know how to talk about it or solve their problem.

2. Communication is crucial in marriage. It's the lifeblood of a marriage relationship. Effective communication helps us avoid problems. It is the key to harmony in marriage.

3. If your group has trouble coming up with barriers, suggest a few of these: lack of communication skills, selfishness, isolation, loss of hope, distractions, disappointment, fear, pride, unresolved conflict, career pressures, children, lack of proper priorities, anger, busy lifestyle, different needs, holding of grudges.

4. Men generally do not communicate their emotions as readily as women. They tend to communicate facts and opinions, and prefer to "get to the bottom line" of a discussion, rather than connecting emotionally. Men tend to be concise and to the point, and women tend to desire more detail.

Be sure to keep the discussion on this question focused on the different communication styles of men and women. Some may want to discuss whether men and women are born with these differences or whether these are learned behaviors. That is not a critical issue for this discussion.

8. She was too concerned with all the work that needed to be done and forgot that her greatest priority should be to listen to Jesus. While her intent was only to serve, her priorities were misplaced.

Attention HomeBuilders Leaders

FamilyLife invites you to register your HomeBuilders group. Your registration connects you to the HomeBuilders Leadership Network, a worldwide movement of couples who are using HomeBuilders to strengthen marriages and families in their communities. You'll receive the latest news about HomeBuilders and other ministry opportunities to help strengthen marriages and families in your community. As the HomeBuilders Leadership Network grows, we will offer additional resources such as online training, prayer requests, and chat with authors. There is no cost or obligation to register; simply go to www.homebuildersgroup.com.

Session Two:
Making Your Relationship a Priority

Objectives

To develop positive communication patterns, you must make your marriage relationship a priority.

In this session, couples will...

- examine their need to make their relationship a higher priority.

- learn practical ways to set priorities.

- apply these principles to their own marriages.

Notes and Tips

1. Since this is the second session, your group members have probably warmed up a bit to each other, but may not yet feel free to be completely open and honest about their relationship. Don't force the issue, but continue encouraging couples to attend and to complete their projects.

2. You may wish to have extra study guides and Bibles for those who didn't bring theirs.

3. If someone joins the group for the first time in this session, give a brief summary of the main points of Session One.

Also, be sure to introduce those who do not know each other. You may want to have each new couple answer a question from the first Warm-Up exercise from Session One.

4. Make sure the arrangements for refreshments (if you're planning to have them) are covered.

5. If your group has decided to utilize a prayer list, make sure this is covered.

6. The first Warm-Up in today's session takes a lighthearted look at communication problems within a marriage. Encourage people to have fun with it. As they do, they'll be caricaturing the real communication problems they see without having to reveal any of their own problems.

7. If you told the group during the first session that you'd be asking them to share something they learned from the first HomeBuilders Project, be sure to ask them. This is an important time for you to establish an environment of accountability.

8. For the closing prayer in this session, you may want to ask for a volunteer or two to close the group in prayer. Check ahead of time with a couple of people you think might be comfortable praying aloud.

Commentary

2. If you make the most of your time (Ephesians 5:15-16), you will use it wisely and not waste it on things that are not important. Regarding others as more important than yourself will influence how you use your time and how you make your decisions (Philippians 2:1-4). Song of Songs 7:10-13 speaks of taking delight in each other. This couple spends time together, they desire each other, and they enjoy each other's love.

Note: The numbers that follow correspond to the Blueprints questions of the same numbers in the session.

3. If people have trouble coming up with examples, share the following example:

Each weekday evening, my dad arrived home from work around 5:30 p.m. The four kids would run to greet him, and then he would sit down with my mom and talk for about an hour. What did they talk about? The business. The children. Their relationship. We kids knew we weren't invited, and believe me, we didn't want to be there. But occasionally I would go into the kitchen and watch them through the doorway. I recall some pretty serious times when they were dealing with problems in the family business. Other times I remember laughter or true emotional intimacy. But they always talked.

Today, Barb and I are following their example. The first thing we do each day when I come home from work is head into the living room and talk. We look forward to it each day, and it sets the mood for the rest of the evening. It's an oasis in a hectic day.

8. This may be a difficult area for some people to confront, because in many cases it means cutting back on activities they enjoy or on responsibilities they have committed to. For some, it may mean working fewer hours or taking work home less often. Some may have to choose not to pursue promotions, raises, or new job opportunities. Some may have to cut back on time spent with hobbies or other outside activities. For still others, it means making a conscious effort to put the same type of effort and creativity into their families, even if they can't give as much.

Session Three:

Communication 101

Objectives

Learning to use basic communication skills will enhance understanding within your marriage.

In this session, couples will...

• discuss three basic components of communication.

• apply these concepts to their own marriages.

Notes and Tips

1. Congratulations. With the completion of this session, you will be halfway through this study. It's time for a checkup: How are you feeling? How is the group going? What has worked well so far? What things might you consider changing as you head into the second half?

2. In this session we look at some basics of communication. For some couples this may be old information, while for others it will at least be a reminder of some skills that need to be sharpened. This is simply a time of identifying some areas to begin to work on, not a time to make radical changes.

3. This session includes quite a few principles that may seem very basic, but practicing them in marriage on a consistent basis can be difficult. Any couple with serious communication problems probably struggles with the principles you'll discuss in this session.

4. Remember the importance of starting and ending on time.

5. For the Blueprints question number 5 in this session, there is a "For Extra Impact" note in the margin that suggests a way to enhance this question. If you choose to utilize this idea, you will need to make sure you have flashlights available for each couple in the group.

6. For Extra Impact: Consider using the following activity in place of the Wrap-Up in the book: Choose two couples to role-play the conversations in these situations. You might have them first present the way most couples might react naturally, and then have them present a conversation based on the components of good communication that you've studied in this session. After the role-plays, have the group discuss the positives and negatives of the communication that took place, suggesting ways of communication that would better promote understanding and strengthen the relationship.

7. You might make some notes right after the meeting to help you evaluate how things went. To help you focus, ask yourself questions such as: Did everyone participate? Is there anyone that I should make a special effort to follow up with before the next session?

8. As a model to the group, it is important that you complete the HomeBuilders Project before each session.

Commentary

2. The tongue can't be tamed. It wields power much like a bit does to direct a horse and a rudder does to guide a ship. It is like a fire spreading its influence to all areas.

Note: The numbers that follow correspond to the Blueprints questions of the same numbers in the session.

3. You might want to mention the Warm-Up question in which the group members told about what attracted them to their spouses. Ask, "How does it make you feel when you hear your spouse talk about those things that are attractive to him or to her?"

7. Most of us want to talk rather than listen. It's hard not to interrupt with comments or feedback. We may get busy, impatient, distracted, disinterested, and selfish. Or we become so preoccupied with the issues going on in our own lives that we don't take the time to think of another person.

9. Mention the following only if your group has trouble coming up with responses: ridiculing what your spouse says; shrugging it off like it doesn't matter; talking too much yourself; becoming defensive; becoming too analytical; trying to find a solution too quickly; changing the subject.

10. Again, suggest the following only if your group has trouble coming up with a good list: giving your spouse your full attention, making good eye contact, allowing your spouse to speak without interruption, asking probing and uncritical questions to draw your spouse out, giving appropriate touch, showing empathy, being approachable.

Feedback can consist of clarifying questions such as, "What did you mean when you said…" Summary questions are also valuable: "Of all that you just said, what do you most want me to understand?"

Session Four:
"Closing the Loop" in Conflict

Objectives

Resolving conflict requires taking the initiative to mend the relationship.

In this session, couples will...

- understand that conflict is inevitable in marriage.

- discuss their need to make a conscious effort to resolve a conflict once it begins.

- discuss four steps in resolving conflict—preparing one's heart, loving confrontation, offering forgiveness, and regaining trust.

- apply these principles to their own marriages.

Notes and Tips

1. We've found that the very act of discussing conflict sometimes causes conflict! It will be important for you as group leader to set a relaxed and accepting atmosphere. The Warm-Up should help you establish this.

2. For this session, the primary focus is the need for couples to make an effort to resolve conflict. The last part of this session introduces a biblical pattern for resolving conflict which we call "Closing the Loop." We recommend that you read through the material in Session Four before leading this session so that you will understand the entire process of closing the loop.

3. Conflict is a part of every relationship. The process of "closing the loop" was birthed in the counseling room and has grown up with hundreds of couples, just like those in your study, who needed to learn how to get through times of conflict. Tell your group members that this process is a tool that can help resolve conflict. Encourage them to try it out. You might want to pick up a copy of *Dr. Rosberg's Do-It-Yourself Relationship Mender* for a comprehensive look at how this process works.

4. As you talk about preparing hearts during the "closing the loop" process, remind couples how important it is to bring God into the midst of their communication. Prayer and Bible study can help greatly in the resolution of our conflicts.

5. The offering of forgiveness is a key to healing hurts. God's plan is to bring these times of forgiveness into our marriages.

6. By this time, group members should be getting more comfortable with each other. For prayer at the end of this session, you may want to give anyone an opportunity to pray by asking the group to finish a sentence that goes something like this: *"Lord, I want to thank you for _____."* Be sensitive to anyone who may not feel comfortable doing this.

Commentary

1. Suggest the following if your group has trouble coming up with ideas: lack of communication, different perspectives of conflict, tendency to avoid it, lack of poor role models growing up, poor role models in the media.

Note: The numbers that follow correspond to the Blueprints questions of the same numbers in the session.

3. Anger often prevents conflicts from being resolved peacefully. Either those angry feelings are expressed with hostility and pain—as a weapon—or they are buried deep within the heart, allowing bitterness and resentment to grow. True intimacy will never be experienced until the loop is closed.

4. Some factors are pride, guilt, laziness, fear, anger, hurt feelings, fatigue, and ignorance of how to resolve conflict. For example, pride can keep a person from taking the initiative to resolve a conflict, rationalizing that he will wait until the other person humbles himself first.

6. Ephesians 4:26-27—When you "let the sun go down while you are still angry," you are making a conscious choice to harbor that anger in your heart rather than attempting to resolve the conflict. You need to resolve conflicts quickly; otherwise that suppressed anger will allow bitterness to take root in your heart.

8. Entering a conflict seeking to win or to prove the other person wrong, only makes it worse. These Scriptures call for humility and setting aside the desire for revenge.

10. A wise tongue can bring healing by explaining how you feel in a situation, asking what your mate needs you to do, and using "I" statements such as, "I'm really feeling upset by this situation, and I need to talk it out with you."

11. God was so concerned about resolving the "conflict" that existed between him and his creation that he made the greatest possible sacrifice to offer forgiveness. That's the kind of forgiveness we're to have toward others, including our spouses.

Session Five:
Communicating Through the Trials of Life

Objectives

God can use you to encourage your spouse during times of trial. In this session, couples will...

- think about the trials they have already experienced and will face in the future.

- discuss their need to turn to God for strength.

- discover how they can encourage each other and improve communication during trials.

Notes and Tips

1. This session will help couples acknowledge a fact that many attempt to avoid—trials are inevitable. Many marriages struggle or break up because the couples are unable to withstand trials in their lives. Humans don't like thinking about problems and trials, and as a result they fail to think ahead and anticipate the trials they will inevitably face. Then, when the trials come, couples turn away from each other rather than clinging to each other for strength.

2. Some couples, as they work through this session, will think, "We don't have many problems...we are blessed." Others will hear couples talk about their trials and think, "Is that all they worry about? Boy, are we in trouble!" Encourage the couples to realize that everyone has different needs, and none of them are insignificant.

3. During times of loss, trials may seem unbearable. During times of major change, people may feel they'll never get through it. If people in your group are struggling with these major trials, be sensitive to their needs and remind them that God will sustain them.

4. If you have a regular prayer time at the end of your session, ask couples to share what trials they're currently facing so that the group can pray together about them. This will help bond the group and demonstrate how encouragement from other people can help during trials.

5. If you're doing this study without using the Wrap-Up section, you might want to consider using that section for this session. It helps couples walk through four principles for dealing with times of trial in their lives.

6. As the leader of a small group, one of the best things you can do for your group is to pray specifically for each member. Why not take some time to pray as you prepare for this session?

Commentary

1. One problem is that many of us don't have the right attitude about trials. We don't like to think about pain; we know that we'll face trials, but we would rather not think about it. Also, many of us simply don't know how to deal with the trials when they come.

Note: The numbers that follow correspond to the Blueprints questions of the same numbers in the session.

2. Trials drive some couples toward each other and toward a greater dependency upon God. With many others, trials intensify any pressure they already are feeling in a relationship. Trials may also work to drive a wedge between a husband and wife; they seek to deal with the problem on their own rather than together.

6. Note that each passage presents part of God's perspective about our trials. God uses them for our good (Romans 8:28), they test our faith and cause us to glorify Christ as we maintain our love for him (1 Peter 1:3-9), and he gives us his Spirit as a blessing (1 Peter 4:12-14).

8. First Corinthians 10:13 and Philippians 4:12-13 assure us that God provides the strength we need to handle any situation. (It's interesting to note that Paul was in prison when he wrote Philippians.) Second Corinthians 1:3-4 let us know of God's comfort during trials.

10. Rejoicing in God despite suffering demonstrates your belief in God's sovereignty. Praying demonstrates your dependence on God and your belief that God will respond.

Session Six:
Achieving Spiritual Intimacy

Objectives

The best and deepest level of communication is achieved when you seek God together.

In this session, couples will...

- consider the need to seek God together in their marriage.

- evaluate their present level of spiritual intimacy.

- make plans to continue working on spiritual intimacy as they have during this study.

Notes and Tips

1. This session presents the key to the entire area of marital communication. Marriage is a relationship of three, not two. Compromise really isn't the answer; obedience to God is. When a man and a woman are both growing in their vertical relationships with God, the horizontal relationship between them comes together as well. This session draws on God's Word to show us just how important it is to be "one in heart and mind" in our marriages.

2. While this HomeBuilders Couples Series has great value, people are likely to gradually return to previous patterns of living unless they commit to a plan for carrying on the progress made. During this final session of the course, encourage couples to take specific steps beyond this series to keep their marriages growing. For example, you may want to challenge couples who have developed the habit of a "date night" during the course of this study to continue this practice. Also, you may want the group to consider doing another study from this series.

3. Near the end of this study, a "For Extra Impact" activity suggests having couples start on the Bible study in the HomeBuilders Project. This is to encourage them to do Bible study together as a couple, whether or not they continue with another HomeBuilders group. If you don't have time for that activity, encourage couples to do the Bible study at the same time they've been setting aside for the HomeBuilders Projects. And offer to help them find Bible study resources for continuing study if they need it.

Commentary

3. It's easy for a Christian couple to develop poor habits in relating to each other if they do not know how to walk in obedience to God on a continual basis.

Note: The numbers that follow correspond to the Blueprints questions of the same numbers in the session.

4. Suggest some of the following if your group doesn't come up with something similar: We would clothe ourselves with compassion, kindness, humility, gentleness and patience. We would bear with each other and forgive each other. We would "put on love." We would do everything to please

Jesus. Such attitudes and actions couldn't help but improve our marriage relationships.

5. It's important to regularly point each other to God. We've done this by praying together, for example. Another thing that we've done in our marriage is to communicate with each other about what God is doing in our lives. From early in our Christian experience, we've asked each other, "Tell me what you are learning." This has begun rich, intimate conversations which have knit our hearts together.

6. Many couples allow their time to be filled with other pursuits: hobbies, family activities, and especially television. Another typical reason is that many spouses wait for the other to take the lead in this area. Also, it's important to realize that this is a spiritual battle—Satan wants to keep you from doing the one thing that will cement your relationship more than anything else.

7. These two actions may be the most important disciplines a couple can build into their marriage. It will revolutionize a couple because they will draw closer to each other as they draw closer to God.

Prayer Requests

Notes

Prayer Requests

Notes

Prayer Requests

Notes

IMPROVING COMMUNICATION IN YOUR MARRIAGE

Prayer Requests

Notes

Prayer Requests

Exciting Resources for Your Adult Ministry!

The Dirt on Learning
Thom & Joani Schultz

This thought-provoking book explores what Jesus' Parable of the Sower says about effective teaching *and* learning. Readers will rethink the Christian education methods used in their churches and consider what really works. Use the video training kit to challenge and inspire your entire ministry team and set a practical course of action for Christian education methods that really *work!*

ISBN 0-7644-2088-7   Book Only
ISBN 0-7644-2152-2   Video Training Kit

The Family-Friendly Church
Ben Freudenburg with Rick Lawrence

Discover how certain programming can often short-circuit your church's ability to truly strengthen families—and what you can do about it! You'll get practical ideas and suggestions featuring profiles of real churches. It also includes thought-provoking application worksheets that will help you apply the principles and insights to your own church.

ISBN 0-7644-2048-8

Disciple-Making Teachers
Josh Hunt with Dr. Larry Mays

This clear, practical guide equips teachers of adult classes to have impact—and produce disciples eager for spiritual growth and ministry. You get a Bible-based, proven process that's achieved results in churches like yours—and comes highly recommended by Christian leaders like Dr. Bruce Wilkinson, Findley Edge, and Robert Coleman. Discover what needs to happen before class through preparation, in class during teaching, and after class in service to turn your adult classes into disciple groups.

ISBN 0-7644-2031-3

Extraordinary Results From Ordinary Teachers
Michael D. Warden

Now both professional *and* volunteer Christian educators can teach as Jesus taught! You'll explore the teaching style and methods of Jesus and get clear and informed ways to deepen your teaching and increase your impact! This is an essential resource for every teacher, youth worker, or pastor.

ISBN 0-7644-2013-5

Discover our full line of children's, youth, and adult ministry resources at your local Christian bookstore, or write: Group Publishing, P.O. Box 485, Loveland, CO 80539. www.grouppublishing.com

$\mathcal{S}$ince attending a FamilyLife Marriage Conference, the Martins' love really shows...

Mommy
x x do x x x o
o o x
Daddy
x y so x o o o y
x x o x

But who's keeping score?

FAMILYLIFE MARRIAGE CONFERENCE
Get away for a "Weekend to Remember"!

Chalk one up for your marriage! Get away to a FamilyLife Marriage Conference for a fun, meaningful weekend together. Learn how to understand your mate, build your marriage, and much more.

**To register or receive more information,
visit www.familylife.com or call 1-800-FL-TODAY.**

FAMILYLIFE™
Bringing Timeless Principles Home

"FamilyLife Today" radio programs have...

Principles to help strengthen your marriage
and ways to love your mate from your

Soul

Advice for parents of both preschoolers and adolescents—
it's sure to help Mom and

Pop

Practical, biblical teaching to build your home
on Christ, the true

ROCK

Insights from host Dennis Rainey and co-host Bob Lepine
on a wide variety of family issues—lots of good

Talk

"FamilyLife Today"—A great format for your family!

For broadcast times call your local Christian radio station or
visit www.familylife.com. Tune in today!

FAMILYLIFE
T·O·D·A·Y

THE ROSBERGS
AMERICA'S
FAMILY COACHES

Dr. Gary & Barbara Rosberg

Newest Release!
The Five Love Needs of Men and Women
(Tyndale)

Written to men from Barb and to women from Gary, this brilliant approach is an excellent guide to understanding the greatest love needs of your mate. A must-read for all!

Do-It-Yourself Relationship Mender
(Focus on the Family/Tyndale)

If you've got a pulse, you've got conflict. This book is a proven plan for mending fractured relationships and strengthening healthy ones.

Guard Your Heart
(Multnomah)

Guard Your Heart is a biblical call for men to be on guard against obvious and subtle moral challenges. This book is THE answer for men today!

America's Family Coaches on the air!

Hear the Rosbergs every weekday on their one-hour program, "America's Family Coaches…LIVE!" as they tackle real life issues and coach families on how to have intimate, meaningful relationships. Also tune in for their one-minute daily features. For a listing of radio stations broadcasting the Rosbergs' programs, call 1-888-ROSBERG.

www.americasfamilycoaches.com

For more information on the ministries of America's Family Coaches, contact us at:

2540 106th Street, Suite 101 • Des Moines, IA 50322
1-888-ROSBERG • (515) 334-7482

1/2/63

Does Your Church Offer Marriage Insurance?

Great marriages don't just happen—husbands and wives need to nurture them. They need to make their marriage relationship a priority.

That's where the newly revised HomeBuilders Couples Series® can help! The series consists of interactive 6- to 7-week small group studies that make it easy for couples to really open up with each other. The result is fun, non-threatening interactions that build stronger Christ-centered relationships between spouses—and with other couples!

Whether you've been married for years, or are newly married, this series will help you and your spouse discover timeless principles from God's Word that you can apply to your marriage and make it the best it can be!

The HomeBuilders Couples Series Leader Guide gives you all the information and encouragement you need to start and lead a dynamic HomeBuilders small group.

HomeBuilders
leader
Guide
Starting and Leading Your Small Group

FAMILYLIFE

Drew and Kit Coons
with David Boehi

The HomeBuilders Couples Series includes these life-changing studies:

Building Teamwork in Your Marriage

Building Your Marriage

Building Your Mate's Self-Esteem

Growing Together in Christ

Improving Communication in Your Marriage

Making Your Remarriage Last

Mastering Money in Your Marriage

Overcoming Stress in Your Marriage

Resolving Conflict in Your Marriage

And check out the HomeBuilders Parenting series!

Building Character in Your Children

Establishing Effective Discipline
   for Your Children

Guiding Your Teenagers

Helping Your Chidlren Know God

Improving Your Parenting

Raising Children of Faith

Look for the **HomeBuilders Couples SerieS and HomeBuilders Parenting Series** at your favorite Christian supplier or write:

Group

3 4711 00176 4564

P.O. Box 485, Loveland, CO 80539-0485.
www.grouppublishing.com

FAMILYLIFE™
Bringing Timeless Principles Home

www.familylife.com